W9-CBR-798

Mining and Farming in Minecraft

By Josh Gregory

Published in the United States of America by
Cherry Lake Publishing
Ann Arbor, Michigan
www.cherrylakepublishing.com

Reading Adviser: Marla Conn, Read With Me Now
Photo Credits: Images by James Zeiger

Library of Congress Cataloging-in-Publication Data has been filed and is available
at catalog.loc.gov

Cherry Lake Publishing would like to acknowledge the work of the Partnership for
21st Century Learning. Please visit *www.p21.org* for more information.

Printed in the United States of America
Corporate Graphics

Table of Contents

Mining will earn you gold. You can use this valuable material to make armor, weapons, and more!

Be Prepared

Resources are the key to any successful *Minecraft* adventure. It doesn't matter if you're building, fighting, or just exploring the world. You'll need plenty of **materials** to succeed. This means it's important to get good at mining and farming. These skills will help you make sure you never run out of the important items you need.

Sometimes you will come across abandoned mines underground as you explore and create your own mines. These areas often contain valuable loot!

Supplies from Underground

Underground mines are the best places to find materials for building. They also have the things you need to **craft** weapons and other gear. These areas are full of stone and metal. They have plenty of coal. You will need this important material to craft torches and fuel your **furnace**.

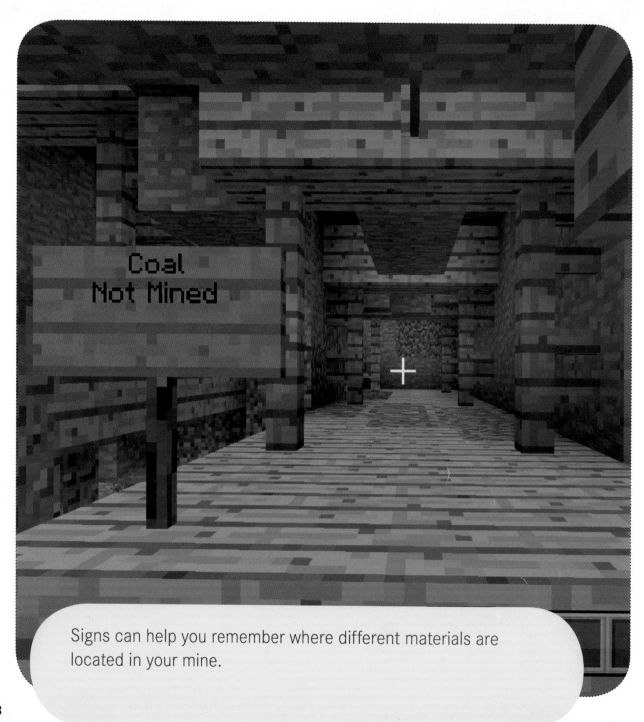

Coal
Not Mined

Signs can help you remember where different materials are located in your mine.

Digging Deep

You can start mining by searching for a cave entrance. You can also just start digging down from any point in the world. Use torches to light the way as you dig. You won't be able to see without them! Another good idea is to place wooden signs along your tunnels. This will tell you how to get back home if you get lost.

Lighting the Way

Always be sure to carry plenty of torches when you are mining. Placing them doesn't only light up a room. It also keeps monsters from **spawning**!

Finding a bunch of diamonds underground is one of the most exciting things that can happen while mining.

Rare Resources

Keep digging your mine deeper and deeper. You probably won't find much near the surface. The best materials are all located deep underground. You might even find rare materials such as diamonds and gold if you get deep enough. Eventually you will reach blocks that you can't dig through. This is **bedrock**. It is the lowest point of the *Minecraft* world.

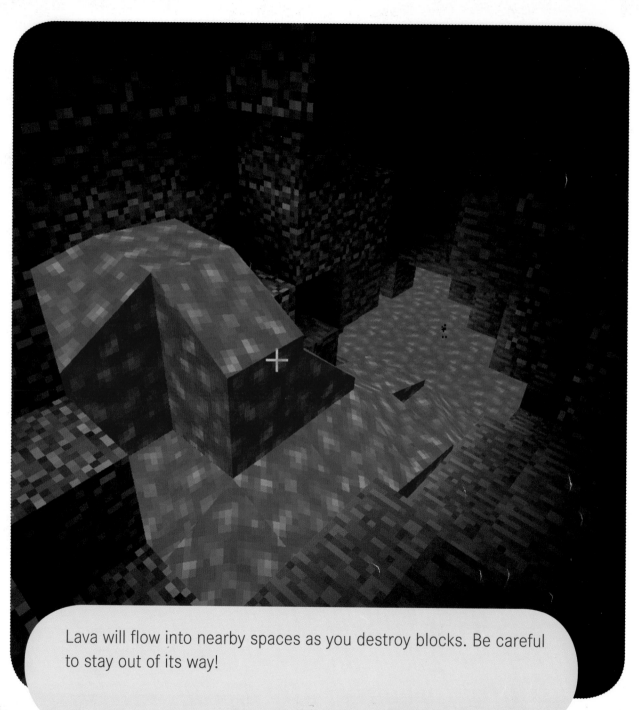

Lava will flow into nearby spaces as you destroy blocks. Be careful to stay out of its way!

Watch Out!

Mining can be dangerous work. Move slowly as you dig. This will help you keep an eye out for trouble. You might suddenly find yourself above a deep pit. Don't fall in! You might also find streams of lava. Don't touch it. It will burn your character. Monsters are another danger. Always carry a sword so you can fight them off.

Farming is a lot less dangerous than mining!

A Farm Full of Food

Farming is another great way to gather useful items. You can grow all kinds of vegetables and other foods. Potatoes, carrots, and melons are just a few examples. These foods will keep your character from getting too hungry. Hungry characters cannot run or heal. Characters that get too hungry can even die!

Combining Crops

You can combine the crops you raise on your farm to create new foods. Growing wheat and sugar will help you make cakes. Cocoa beans can be added to wheat to make chocolate chip cookies. Try out different recipes for yourself!

Land that is ready for planting looks different from regular dirt blocks.

Preparing and Planting

You need a few tools to start growing crops. First, craft a **hoe**. Use the hoe on a block of dirt. Now that block is ready for planting. Some plants start as seeds. These include wheat, melons, and pumpkins. Simply place the seeds on the hoed dirt. Other plants do not use seeds. Place a potato on the dirt if you want to grow a potato plant. A carrot will grow a carrot plant. Sugarcane, cocoa beans, and beets can also be planted this way.

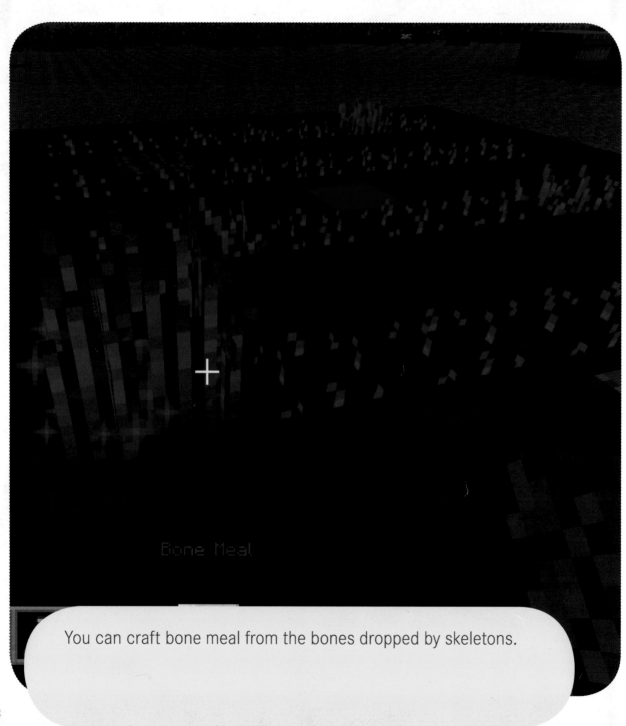

Bone Meal

You can craft bone meal from the bones dropped by skeletons.

Growing Up

Your plants will need sunlight to grow. Water is also important. Don't pour buckets of water right on the crops. Instead, dig a hole and pour water near the crops. The crops will get wet as long as they are four blocks or less away from the water block.

Faster Farming

Are your crops growing too slowly? Place some torches nearby. They will keep getting light even at night. This helps them grow faster! Sprinkling an item called bone meal on your crops will also speed up their growth.

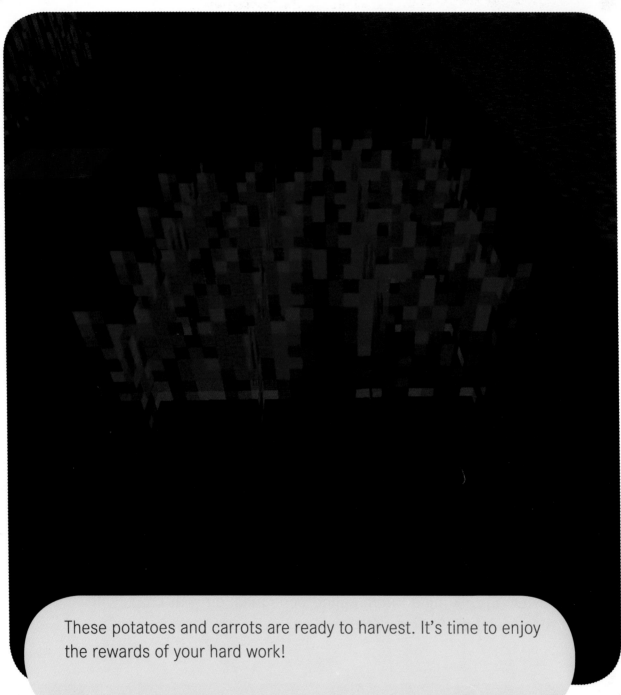

These potatoes and carrots are ready to harvest. It's time to enjoy the rewards of your hard work!

Collecting the Rewards

You can **harvest** your plants once they are done growing. Simply press the Use button when you are near the plant. Your food will fall on the ground so you can pick it up. The plant will be destroyed when you harvest it. This means you will need to plant a new one to grow more crops. What will you grow next?

Glossary

bedrock (BED-rahk) the material that makes up the lowest point of the *Minecraft* world.

craft (KRAFT) make or create

furnace (FUR-niss) in *Minecraft*, a device that uses heat to change certain materials into other materials

harvest (HAR-vist) to gather ripe crops

hoe (HOH) a gardening tool with a long handle and a flat blade that is used to prepare soil for planting

materials (muh-TEER-ee-uhlz) items you need for a particular project or activity

resources (REE-sors-iz) things that are of value or use

spawning (SPAWN-ing) when players, enemies, or other characters appear in the *Minecraft* world

Find Out More

Books

Jelley, Craig. *Minecraft: Guide to Creative*. New York: Del Rey, 2017.

Milton, Stephanie. *Minecraft Essential Handbook*. New York: Scholastic, 2015.

Milton, Stephanie. *Minecraft: Guide to Exploration*. New York: Del Rey, 2017.

Web Sites

Minecraft
https://minecraft.net/en
At the official *Minecraft* Web site, you can learn more about the game or download a copy of the PC version.

Minecraft Wiki
https://minecraft.gamepedia.com/Minecraft_Wiki
Minecraft's many fans work together to maintain this detailed guide to the game.

Index

About the Author

Josh Gregory is the author of more than 125 books for kids. He has written about everything from animals to technology to history. A graduate of the University of Missouri–Columbia, he currently lives in Chicago, Illinois.